तुम खुश रहो
रहो भीतर, जीयो बाहर
प्रतिभा जैन

SOURCE OF INSPIRATION

My inner being bows in reverence to Antrmana Guruji.

You are a blessing for the creation, a divine fragrance of conduct, your love is infinite, indescribable, immeasurable. With zeal, enthusiasm and affection, you distribute nectar in life, shower eternal joy. The uninterrupted flow of showers of your intelligence and brilliance has flooded the deserts of human life and is creating new swastikas on the white sky of humanity.

You have taken a deep dive into the ocean of sadhana and the sadhana is attaining supernaturality and grandeur.

Countless gold coins of pure thoughts are being distributed…

Respectable pearls of love are scattering like this…

The fragrance of the fragrance of the fragrance maker man,
anointed with sadhana…

Humanity enlightened by waves of special will power

A waterfall of joy is flowing

The strings of the sleeping veena got plucked…

The dormant possibilities of consciousness took hold…

Smiles pouring from every pore,
joy overflowing from the heart,
freshness all the time,
amazing effect in the eyes,
restrained emotionality,
charming style,
Saraswati's glow in the throat,
face glowing with satisfaction and vigor.

You, a deep sensation,
a unique feeling.

Pratibha Jain

मन की बात
Mann Ki Baat

This vast universe is contained in nothingness. Whatever sprouts from nothingness, silence, and stillness is auspicious. Life is the development of dormant possibilities, introduction to oneself, life is a journey, journey is a mirror, in which the picture of a person's personality comes out.

In the search of the eternal, on the path of truth, let the journey of life become a mirror, realizing this truth, by establishing oneself as a laboratory, by going through many tests, surveys, by becoming a constantly vigilant guard in the field of thoughts and feelings, let the pearls of experiences and feelings that have been collected become helpful in awakening the inner awareness, let the inner self be illuminated and in that light, we can illuminate ourselves.

Words are limited, feelings are limitless. My endeavour is to give meaningful expression to my originality and sensitivity. The source of life's shine and fragrance is within, not outside. My ambition is to develop a stable, deep personality, and by establishing friendship with oneself, the doors of world friendship can be opened.

Even if the flow of life is adverse, a clear thinking makes everything favorable. Whatever imbalance, pollution and disorder there is in life, we should be able to solve it with our positive thinking and feelings, this is the effort in this creation. Live in the world and the world should not reside in the mind.

We ourselves are the best book in the world, we should learn to read ourselves. We should develop such a state of mind that our decisions and our distances cannot be created, this is the feeling.

It is true that sorrow comes in life, but the art of living is that we overcome sorrow with a smile and come out of it. The purpose of this creation is that we can do this. To be happy, it is necessary to follow some rules and principles of life. It is also important to know yourself, understand others, control over the mind. The essence of this work is that we can move on the path of truth, meditation and self-upliftment and attain silent bliss.

"Tum Khush Raho" is not just a name, it is a life mantra, a way of life. This creation "Tum Khush Raho" is a prayer in itself, a pure flow of emotions from the heart. My heart is full of love and happiness, I want to share what I have. To be sad, to be disappointed

There is a disease, a crime in the self. To be happy is to live every moment in the present with a feeling of gratitude. Only by being happy can we inherit happiness.

This creation is a deep feeling, a powerful experience. The desire is that the shades of the countless colors of its thoughts can make the difficulties in life easy. Life should become conscious, the sleeping mind should wake up and we should be able to listen to the inner music of life.

Throughout our lives we search for someone separate from ourselves and eventually lose ourselves. We must keep ourselves safe and find in life what we exist to find. Meditation and silence are the paths.

You are close to us, now our small sky and small piece of land seem infinite to us. With your influence, power and blessings, I become bodiless and wish for liberation.

Pratibha Jain

BEST WISHES!

Mrs. Pratibha Ji, who is endowed with a remarkable talent, has understood the essence of the practice of Videha while being in the body. The work you have done through your writings to spread goodwill, love and friendship towards the family, society and country by assimilating the style of living a balanced life in different situations of life like the lotus that grows in water and mud through meditation, which is the incomparable step of witnessing the transformation of the soul, and by assimilating the style of living a balanced life in happiness, sorrow, respect and insult, like the lotus that grows in water and mud, is praiseworthy.

What do we do all our life-

"We collect things."

"We build houses."

"We fill our coffers."

And you keep losing yourself.

My best wishes and blessings to the readers of 'Tum Khush Raho' are that this work will serve as a guide in life.

Conscience

||Acharya Prasanna Sagar||

CONTENTS

(1)

FORMULA'S OF LIFE

Life is multifaceted.

Life is a story of effort,

the answer to every difficult question of life

is found in life itself.

Let us live in awareness, not in burden.

LIFE IS A SACRIFICE

Life has no color of its own, we who You can fill colours as you like. Life is a blank paper. Life

Every day, every moment we fill that paper with songs.

Life is a blessing, a prasad, a gift – we should respect it. Life is a yagya, we should sacrifice our evils in it. Life is introduction to oneself. It is prayer.

There should be no worries in life, there should be contemplation, there should be no options, there should be determination.

There should be no tension, there should be

balance, there should be no lethargy, there should

be awakening.

ART OF LIVING

The meaning of life lies in the art of living. Life is contained in the way of living. Life is an echo – 'what you give will come back to you'. Life is an opportunity – be alert, don't miss it. Life is a challenge – accept it, face it. Life is a vision – observation without reaction is required. Life is a message. Understand it. Life is a journey, journey is a mirror – a picture of a person's personality comes out in it.

TRUE-FALSE

If we live a life based on truth, and not in lies and pretense, then our life will be natural, simple but powerful and if we live a false life, a life of pretense, tell a hundred lies to hide one lie, then it is certain that there will be difficulties in our life and our life will be weak. Cheating ourselves, deceiving others as well, only misunderstanding. Small lies, small sorrows bring bigger lies and bigger sorrows in life. A lie does not last, it is helpless, a lie has no legs.

PRESENT MOMENT

Compete with yourself every moment in life, move ahead and enjoy victory. The present is enough to be happy. We should not sow the seeds of sorrow, pain and despair in the present moment. Because the seed of sorrow will only bring sorrow. Our present moment should be positive, full of divinity. Thoughts, feelings should be noble and high. Living in the present moment is a wise decision, it is respect for time. Today's present moment will give birth to tomorrow. Today, right now, be joyful in this very moment, stay joyful - the future will be joyful.

WANT TO BE HAPPY

Problems increase problems, they do not solve them. Happiness increases happiness, and problems also get solved. One has to be happy in every situation, one has to be happy every moment. One has to be happy today, right here and now. Be happy in your own being- if you are alone then be happy- one should not wait for anyone's company. If someone is with you then be happy, participate in everyone's happiness. Be cooperative. One needs a reason to be sad, but there is no need for any reason to be happy. We should make being happy our life mantra. Only by being happy can we become winners in life.

WORDS OF RESTRAINT

Wherever you have to speak, speak with restraint, speak sweetly, speak as per the need. Where it is necessary to speak, do not remain silent, do not remain quiet, this is wrong. We should know how to call wrong as wrong, otherwise things can get worse. Where there is no need, remain quiet, do not get entangled in useless arguments. Do not speak just for the sake of speaking, maintain silence here. Speaking should not become our disease, it should become our treatment.

LIVE AND LET LIVE

Every living being has a right to live, we cannot snatch anyone's right to live. We have to protect our own right to live. Life is a very beautiful experience, a mystery, experience the beauty of life, feel it. We should take care that others should not have any kind of pain or sorrow because of us. We should feel love and compassion towards every living being. Live life with love, know it through experience. Know yourself, understand yourself but do not limit yourself to yourself. Spread yourself, share love.

LIVE IN TODAY

Life is today, right now and right here. We have to live in the present, we have to live the present. We can sow the seeds of the future only in the present. We should not ignore the present moment in life, we should appreciate and respect the present moment. The present moment is the decisive moment of life. Living in the past and the future is slavery, it wastes time and energy. We can be independent only by living in the present. It is in the present moment that our fortune improves and deteriorates. We should give meaning to the present moment.

FLOW

Flowing water is clean. Let us become a flowing stream, not stagnant water. Life is the name of change. Wherever we are, whatever we are, from there only a meaningful direction of life can be decided. There are many positive aspects in life, we can start from anywhere. We should not get stuck in happiness, nor get lost in sadness. Nothing stays here, everything is changeable. There may be stagnation in life, but we should not stop, we should keep moving.

DON'T RUSH

Do your work, don't worry about the result. Work is a seed, be careful and alert while sowing. The seed of sorrow will bring sorrow only. Tears will bring tears only. Happiness brings happiness. Every step taken in the right direction is fruitful. We have to make hundred percent effort. But don't be impatient or in a hurry, haste takes more time. Sow the seed, add fertilizer and water and wait. The seed will break, fruits will come, but we cannot speed up this process. This is the work of nature, it will happen according to the law of nature.

SMILE IS A BLESSING

Smile is a divine blessing to us. Express it. Smile in itself is the biggest medicine, a drug. Smile and stay healthy. Smile makes us beautiful and attractive. Smile creates magnetic qualities in us. If you want to remain comfortable, smile. When we don't have an answer to any question, then smile. Smile when you complain. If you want to make someone yours, then smile; if you want to become yours, then smile. Smile when you meet, smile when you bid farewell. Smile is victory. There should not be emptiness or bitterness in the smile, it should be the color of love and friendship only.

LOSE, DON'T GIVE UP

Every success story is a story of great failure. Do not avoid failure, do not be afraid, failure teaches a great lesson in life, the treasure of experience also increases. Lose, but do not accept defeat. Do not lose heart- keep an eye on the next step. Failure teaches us to struggle. It teaches us to fight the challenge. This brings perseverance in life. It brings determination. Learn to convert failure into success. Learn to convert unfavorable conditions into favorable ones.

TAKE ADVICE CAREFULLY

Taking advice from someone is a very important thing. Take advice from Krishna, not Shakuni. Do not take advice from everyone. We should not go to anyone for advice just because of convenience and information. This is not right. Take advice only from successful and experienced people in their respective fields. Those from whom we seek advice must be our well-wishers. Those who will give us inspired advice. They will not let us feel disappointed. Taking advice from someone is a responsible job, be careful.

STAY STRESS FREE

A restless mind is tension in itself. The simple meaning of tension is that we want to be what we are not. Maintain a balance between stillness and movement in life. Acquisition and renunciation should be balanced. There should be vision, not display. This is relief from tension. We should maintain distance from those who distance us from ourselves. People are there for love, things are there for use. We are living the opposite - this is tension. Relationships are not made only with words, there must be feelings. Learn to remain calm and forgive. There are many ways of cooperation, those who deceive find excuses. We should remain tension-free.

LAZINESS IS GRIEF

Our laziness is the story of our defeat. Laziness is bound to bring sorrow in life. Life is priceless, each moment is precious, luck also results only from hard work. It is not right to keep postponing any matter to tomorrow, life will flow away in the gurgling sound of tomorrow. Do not get lost in dreams. Dreams have to be made true. Seize the time at the right time, do proper time management, planning, coordination. Leave laziness, get up, try. Those who try, never lose. Be honest to yourself. Laziness is deceiving yourself. Wake up, don't make excuses.

BECOME SUCCESSFUL

Do not be afraid of what people say, they keep changing colors like a chameleon. Do not be afraid of 'no', think of 'yes', it will not take long for 'no' to become 'yes'. Work hard to make your dreams come true. Have faith in yourself, keep distance from wrong company, wrong thoughts, and beliefs. Have the courage to call wrong as wrong. Never make a habit of postponing work, do not make excuses. Be comfortable, be stress-free and focus on the goal with a positive attitude. Develop the habit of looking at problems as solutions.

TODAY AND NOW

Live today and now, be happy. Make the present worth living. We have to live today only, there is no other way to live. Don't live under the illusion of tomorrow, this moment is an opportunity. This moment should not go to waste. If you can sing a song today, right now, then don't postpone it for now. Don't postpone laughing every day. Sorrow is not something to be accumulated, make the present happy. Every moment of today is creating tomorrow. A happy tomorrow will not be born from a sad today. Time is born from within us. Whatever be the date, we create our time.

CHANGE IS ACCEPTABLE

Every moment the outside world is changing, every moment everything is changing inside us too. Change, transformation is the truth. Accept it, welcome it. Change happens only in the present. Life gets a new dimension through change. Sometimes there is trouble and obstacles in change but achievement in life also comes from change. Change is not mud, it is a teacher. The mind wants to hold on to small pleasures, that is why change is not easily accepted. We have to welcome the new.

AS IS THE VISION, SO IS THE CREATION

If our focus is on goodness, we will find the world good. Our determination and perspective is the deciding factor. It is up to us whether we live the life of a swan or a crow. We should carve virtues or look at the vices. Our eyes are on the thorn or the flower. By keeping our perspective positive, we can be delighted by the shine and glow of the countless colors and forms of life. We can admire the infinite beauty in it. Our life can smell with the fragrance of love.

AS YOU THINK, SO IS YOUR LIFE

We are all endowed with some special quality and are useful to humanity. Not everything in life is good, but we can see the good in everything. We can have the attitude of accepting the good. When we start seeing the bad in everything, we become that. Whatever feeling we like, we attract the same from the atomic nature.

AS IS THE GRAIN, SO IS THE MIND

The quality of our food, the way of cooking and consuming food, the right time, are definitely very important. The environment around us and our state of mind during meals play a crucial role. It is not right to eat in an atmosphere of violence, excitement, conflict, the mind should be happy and positive at this time. Our food should give us a positive mind, keep us full of vitality. Develop such a mindset. Do not just focus on taste and decoration.

WHERE THERE IS A WILL, THERE IS A WAY

The secret of existence and development of our life is hidden in our will power and determination.

Will power is behind all our positive and creative work. Where there is a will, there is a way, a solution. Our will, desire can also be associated with evil, then it works to destroy. We should always try to keep our thoughts and feelings auspicious so that our will, desire is auspicious. Auspicious feeling becomes resolution. Will is the mother of every invention.

LIKE WHAT YOU GOT

We should like what we have got. Respect it, appreciate it. Be thankful. Feel grateful for what we have got. Feel joy in what we have got, be happy. By liking what we have got, the ability and capacity to get what we like develops. This is the law of nature. So like what we have got and also become entitled to get what we like.

AS PER THE SIGHT, SO IS THE VIEW

Our outlook towards life gives meaning and essence to life. We should search for light and see the goodness. In every situation, we should see flowers and not thorns; we should see light and not darkness. Our outlook decides everything in life. It is because of our special outlook that everyone's world is different even while living in the same world. We should focus on goodness so that goodness can develop in us. We should be positive towards the means of living life; means are for us, not we for the means.

AS YOU THINK, SO IS YOUR FATE

Our thinking is our destiny. We are creating our destiny every moment. We have written our destiny ourselves. Then why should we write sorrow in our destiny? Think meaningfully, think good - whatever you think, the same atoms will be attracted towards us by nature. If you think that this will definitely happen, then it will definitely happen. To achieve destiny, one has to think with awareness, have to think with effort, and then put the thought into action. The destiny of a sleeping person also goes to sleep.

WHAT I HAVE GOT IS ENOUGH

What we have, how much we have, how it is, is important. Our focus should be on this only. We should not focus on what we do not have. Whenever we look at life, we should look at it from a positive perspective. The law of nature is full of justice. We will definitely get what is ours, we should have faith in this and also satisfaction. This is the feeling of acceptance, the feeling of gratitude. This feeling gives birth to happiness and smile in life.

LIKE THE SEED, LIKE THE FRUIT

As the seed so the fruit, if you sow a Babul tree how will you get mangoes. Karma always gives its fruit, yes, there can be a difference in the time between karma and fruit. One has to be alert while sowing the seed, sow the seed in awareness, the fruit will be good. Our thoughts are seeds, it is very important to remain conscious at the level of thoughts. Hence sow the seeds of happiness and peace, sow the seeds of love and joy. Wait patiently, do not hurry. You will definitely get the fruit as per the seed.

LIFE IS A CHOICE EVERY MOMENT

Life is a choice every moment. Choice and decision are very important in life. Ask yourself whether our decision, our choice is taking us towards awakening or towards unconsciousness, keep the result in mind. There should be foresight, there should be foresight. We should be able to understand the long term results of our choice. Our choice builds our life. It determines the direction and condition of life. It creates our destiny. We should be honest towards ourselves and fulfill our responsibilities with honesty.

SMILE THROUGH PROBLEMS

If there is life then there is problem, if there is mind then there is conflict, if there is body then there is illness. But we should consider the problem as a challenge, as a lesson. Problems are like the red light of the traffic, it turns green after a little wait. So we should smile amidst the problem, have some patience. At the time of problem, let there be minimum disturbance on the surface of the mind, like a line drawn on water. So that the problem does not have any negative impact on life or it is minimal.

SENSE OF APPRECIATION

Virtuous people should be praised, respected, their praise is commendable. In life, our focus should not be on faults, shortcomings, weaknesses. By focusing on virtues, we become entitled to acquire those virtues. We become like the subject we focus on. As is the view, so is the view. Goodness brings only goodness. The feeling of accepting virtues should always remain.

PROTECTION OF NATURE

Protection of nature is our protection. It is our responsibility and our duty to follow the rules of nature. We should stay close to nature so that our life remains natural and simple. We should remain fresh and enthusiastic. Only through the protection of nature will we be able to protect our civilization and culture. We should stay in our nature and protect nature.

ATTACHMENT IS SORROW

We need support, we need something to hold on to, we need happiness. If we don't get happiness, then let sadness be fine. We want to remain sad; we want to attract others through sadness. These are negative things. The habit of holding on is attachment. Attachment makes us dependent, unhappy. "I should not let go of my desires, wishes, I should hold on to them, how can I get what I don't have," we remain entangled in these things. This is what we have to understand, attachment is bondage; attachment makes us do things that we don't want to do. We have to break the bondage, come out of sadness, become self-reliant.

LIFE IS CHANGEABLE

Everything is changing every moment, life is changeable, nothing is permanent here, there can be an illusion of stagnancy. We should also live like flowing water, like a river. What is there today will not be there tomorrow, what was there yesterday is not there today. Trying to hold on to any thought, emotion, condition, situation, trying to stop it is futile. No feeling can be the same again and again. Life is new every moment, we should remain fresh.

SOLUTION TO PROBLEM

Life is a problem as well as a solution. We should look at life as a solution. The right understanding of the problem is the solution. The solution is hidden in the problem itself. If there is sadness in life, then ask yourself, why is there sadness? The answer is within us. We are the cause of sadness, that is, we are the problem and we are the solution. If the outlook on life is positive, then life becomes a solution. As soon as the solution is found, the mind starts flowing in one direction in the form of power.

PAIN BECOMES MEDICINE

If there is life then there is pain, we are born with pain. Pain is an integral part of human life. Do not suppress your pain, do not hide it, do not deny it, accept the pain. It is natural, innate. But do not hate the pain, do not make the pain your sorrow. Learn to live in pain, learn to live with the pain, smile in pain. Make pain a medicine. The happiness of life does not decrease due to pain. Night plays a big role in the coming of the day. Pain goes away only after giving the feeling of happiness.

EXPRESSION OF FEELINGS

Language is weak and incapable of expressing emotions. But emotions want expression. When there is too much sorrow, the language of tears is expressed. When there is too much joy, tears are the expression. When emotions are strong, we want to say a lot but we are unable to say anything and when there is nothing to say, we say a lot. Tears of love are very pure, priceless. No song, no poem can be more beautiful than tears of love.

HAPPINESS-SORROW

Happiness and sorrow are two sides of the same coin. Sorrow is the base of happiness, happiness is the result of sorrow. Happiness turns into sorrow and sorrow into happiness in a moment. The line between happiness and sorrow is very thin. So if you don't get what you wanted, don't be sad, it may be that happiness lies in it. If you get what you wanted, don't be very happy, it may become the reason of our sorrow in the future. Maintain stability of mind in happiness and sorrow. Happiness comes with sorrow, sorrow goes after giving happiness

GRATITUDE IS HUMANITY

We should never forget the kindness of others in our lives. Whatever service, hospitality, support others have shown us, we should always have a sense of gratitude, a sense of thanks, a sense of grace for that. Gratitude is the identity of humanity. When we do a favor to someone, we should not expect that he will be grateful to us. Do a favor and leave the rest to nature. There is a saying; do good and throw it in the river. We should always be grateful for the favors of others, never be ungrateful.

HABITS BECOME RITUALS

We should make habits consciously, not unconsciously. We should not make habits like machines. Become the master of your habits, do not let the habits become the master. Become dependent but let freedom remain, do not become dependent. Remain aware. Chant the rosary, but remain your own master. If we are the master, then habits are good, for the slave everything is a hindrance. For the master, freedom. There is nothing like saving yourself by losing yourself.

UNDERSTANDING OF LIFE

Life is not meant for being sad, it is meant for coming out of sadness. If we are sad, then we do not know how to live, we do not understand life. Restraint and Sadhana in life are not difficult or unique things, understand their importance. Without self-restraint and Sadhana, even small goals in life cannot be achieved. Self-restraint and Sadhana are the best efforts. To achieve success in life, we have to walk on the path of self restraint and Sadhana.

(2)

RELATIONSHIP WITH SELF

Loving yourself is the most powerful story in life.

Loving oneself is also the basis of loving the world.

When we come to ourselves,
Recognize your energy and power,
Then the entire existence
welcomes us with open arms.

FRIENDSHIP WITH ONESELF

We can be our own true friends. To get angry is to be our own enemy. To punish ourselves for the mistakes of others is injustice to ourselves. We are taking poison every day. No one else is our enemy, we are becoming our own enemy. No one else is causing us pain, we are causing pain to ourselves. We are responsible, do not put the blame elsewhere. Take your responsibility, do not run away. Cooperate with yourself, express divine qualities by walking on the right path. Be your own friend, stop causing pain to yourself, do not become an obstacle for yourself

BE WITH YOURSELF

Life is a stage. Here everyone has to play many roles simultaneously. We should play all our roles to the best of our ability and capacity. Do the best that we can. There are no retakes in life and every shot has to be made the best. So be conscious every moment in life. Let our dormant possibilities develop in life and let us allow ourselves to become what we have come to be on this earth. Let your support be there, let there be faith in the mind, let there be development of consciousness.

TRAVELER OF JOY

We are the ones who create obstacles for ourselves. We are the ones who stop us, no one else stops us. If we want to be happy, want to be joyful, then who is stopping us? We are the seekers of happiness, love is our nature, then why are we sad? Why do we want to be sad? We should help ourselves, support ourselves. Understand ourselves, choose happiness for ourselves, not sadness, the responsibility is ours. Make yourself better than yourself, and unite yourself with yourself.

SELF SAFETY

Our attitude towards life is our security. We should build and develop our personality within this security. We should not get angry on small things without any reason, we should not remain afraid and we should not resort to lies. Stay away from negative attitude. Do not make excuses in life. Do not live in comparison. We can doubt our point of view, but we must have faith in our joy and happiness.

OWN RESPONSIBILITY

The problem lies in the thought that 'the problem is in others'. The problem is in us, it is from us. We should work on ourselves, take responsibility and work honestly. To look for faults in others is to reduce our own ability. Desiring peace from someone else takes us away from peace. When we stop criticizing others, complaining to others, then our vices will automatically be destroyed. Virtues will develop, we will be empowered.

COMMUNICATE WITH ONESELF

Not every slap in life is a slap, some slaps are blessings. So we have to understand, not react immediately. Which event, situation, person is a blessing in our life, and which is disruptive. Ask yourself, question yourself, be an explorer. Communicate directly with yourself. Do not let your instincts and beliefs become an obstacle. This is freedom. No incarnation from outside will come to awaken us, to communicate with us. We have to awaken the incarnation within us. Light your own lamp.

INDEPENDENCE

We can get only that from others which we want to get. Someone said something wrong. But it is our freedom to give that wrong thing any place in our mind or not. We may not accept those things. We should take only that which is in our interest. We do not have control over others, but we have control over ourselves. We should not make ourselves a vessel of garbage. The world troubles only those who want to be troubled. We should do what God likes.

GIVE YOURSELF A GIFT

There is no need for a reason to be good. Being good is in our nature. Being good makes us feel good. We are what we are, our speech, behaviour and actions will be like that. We should not look for angels in this world, we should become them. We should not think that we will become good when the world becomes good. But we should think that we should become good so that the world becomes good. We should become good and remain so continuously. We should give this gift to ourselves.

BUILDING DREAMS

We should create our dreams ourselves, otherwise someone else will create our dreams in their own way. Then it is possible that we will not be able to remain happy. Choose your own dream, be self-confident and fulfill it. The outline of the dream should be clear in our mind and heart. Let go of useless things, become zero, become light and new. Get free from distortion, make your dreams come true.

ACCEPTED SENTIMENT

Whatever we are, however we are, whatever our circumstances are, favourable or unfavourable, we should see them as they are, accept them as they are. Whatever nature has given us, rejecting it is foolishness, ignorance. Whatever we have got today is the reflection of our own deeds, the result. The feeling of acceptance means accepting your own deeds. Change is possible only through acceptance. Change can happen only consciously. There is satisfaction in the feeling of acceptance, consciousness and effort are the necessary conditions for change.

CONSISTENCY WITH WITNESS

The mind is restless, trembling, endless waves of thoughts and clouds of emotions keep surging and swirling in the mind. The mind gets stuck, wanders, and is restless. If we become aware of the thoughts and emotions coming and going in our mind and can observe them with the attitude of a witness, with the attitude of a spectator, then the instability and restlessness of the mind will diminish, thoughts will keep decreasing. There is no need to evaluate, no reaction. Reaction-free philosophy plays a very effective role in solving the problems of the subconscious mind.

SPREAD HAPPINESS

We are happy and sad because of ourselves. We have received all the sorrows from ourselves. We always keep blaming others. Whatever we spread on others is our sorrow. Always turn within, light your own lamp. Do not try to avoid sorrow, do not get lost in sorrow, be at ease. Accept it but do not welcome it. The effort to give happiness to others creates happiness within us, whatever you share will come back to you. So share happiness, spread happiness, we will be entitled to happiness.

WE ARE THE JUDGE

People say, they say in every situation, their opinion is theirs, our thoughts are ours, we should decide right and wrong ourselves. Borrow any opinion from others as knowledge and understanding. We can get words from others, but not truth. Living happens by ourselves, within ourselves. We should become a well. Not a pond, not a water tank. We should feel the spark of originality from within. We should remove the stones and pebbles within us, water will gush out from within. This will not be borrowed, it will be our own, it will be original.

FEELING OF RICHNESS

Nature has sent us to this earth with some priceless gems, we are definitely rich. We have a sweet smile, which is priceless, it works like a magnet. Our loving gaze is indescribable in itself. Our sweet words can add nectar to life. We can pray from the heart. Wishing well for everyone is a sadhana in itself. We can serve others - this is the feeling of being rich.

A SELF-RESPECTING LIFE

It is not necessary that you always win in a fight with your loved ones. But when the fight is with yourself, then winning becomes necessary. We cannot live after defeating ourselves. Losing to ourselves is the defeat of life, living a life of death. Falling in your own eyes is not self-respect. We should be priceless in our own eyes. God has not made anyone like us. We are special, unique.

JUST SMILE

Laugh and smile in every difficulty, ease, favorable and unfavorable situation of life. Smile and go through every situation. Laughter, smile is a sadhana, a meditation in itself. Smile is in our nature, we should remain in our nature. Storms will come, tempests will come, let them come, let them go, we should just smile. Keep smiling, the picture will be good. Our picture is being made every moment in life, the picture of good upbringing. We cannot escape from this, so smile.

LIVE WITHIN YOURSELF

We argue and reason with others. Arguing with others always raises new questions, and then an endless series of questions continues. There is no result, the mind keeps us entangled in logic and debate. We should argue, reason and question ourselves, not others. Ask the right questions, the answer will come from within. We are the answer, we are the solution. Be calm and silent and find answers from yourself. Live within yourself, live yourself.

PAY ATTENTION TO THINKING

Think only about what is meaningful, don't think about what is useless and meaningless. Hold on to the meaningful and let go of the meaningless. Our thinking is our destiny. Wrong thinking invites wrong events and situations in our life. We should pay attention to our thinking. The thoughts to which we give more time and energy – believe in them, those things will come into our life as reality. First in an invisible form, then in a visible form.

FOCUS ON SELF

We like others to pay attention to us, but we don't like to pay attention to ourselves, to be focused on ourselves. Everyone wants attention from others. But our existence, our nature, wants us to pay attention to ourselves. This is the path to freedom, to liberation. Only by meeting ourselves, by knowing ourselves, can we bring about a radical change in our lives, can we transform them. This is sadhana. Live in faith, live in joy.

LIVE WITHIN YOURSELF

We should keep the being inside us, who we really are, happy and safe. Look at life through our own lens. Create positive feelings for ourselves, in our own way. We should live within ourselves, in our own way. We should be light and stress-free. We should not live as exploiter or exploited. We should connect with ourselves, this is connecting with the universe, connecting with God. We are seeds, we become trees, we become oceans from drops.

SELF OBSERVATION

Observation is a scientific process. Just observation, the process of transformation in seeing itself. We have to observe ourselves. Whatever comes in front of us, we should understand it with neutrality, with equanimity, with awareness. We have to become a witness, a seer. Our neutral observation brings transformation in life. "I am separate from my actions, sins and virtues, good and bad, I am separate from the observer-body, I am separate from the mind." The more we experience this, the more our consciousness will develop. We will be able to see life with neutrality.

MIRACLES IN LIFE

When we accept ourselves completely, a miracle happens in life. We become self-loving, connected to that supreme power. Then love flows spontaneously, towards everyone, everywhere. There is nothing to do, no effort. Discipline becomes a natural part of life. We are filled with self-confidence. Life moves towards self-realization.

WE ARE PRECIOUS

We are priceless. We are God's signature. We should accept ourselves, appreciate ourselves, respect ourselves. He has made us unique, unique and incomparable. Whatever is best, meaningful, we deserve it. Always think good for ourselves, speak good, do good. Make ourselves such that every atom of existence likes us. Everyone, everything around us likes us. Let us get drenched in this happiness, in joy

(3)

RELATIONSHIPS WITH OTHERS

To hurt others is ultimately to hurt oneself.

Here everyone is our own, no one is a stranger,
everyone is a stranger, no one is our own.

Everyone is different, everyone is independent

POWER OF WORDS

It is through words that we relate to others. Words have their own special power, energy. So choose your words very carefully. Our words should become medicine, prayer, prayer for others. Our words should shower nectar, not poison. Our words should be such that we can write them and sign. But in life, we should not get stuck or stray only in the words of others. We should also pay attention to their purpose and feelings. Their negative words should not affect us.

I CAN ONLY GIVE WHAT I HAVE

If we are unhappy within ourselves, we can only give unhappiness to others. The waves of our thoughts and feelings keep radiating from us and reach others in the same form. It is not possible that we are not in love and yet are able to share love with others. So first we should fill ourselves with love, happiness, joy. Then it will reach others without any effort spontaneously. Trying or claiming to give what we do not have is futile, fruitless.

ART OF LISTENING

Speaking is definitely an art, but listening is an even greater art. Those who do not know how to listen, do not know how to speak either. Listening develops the art of speaking. Do not listen only with your ears, listen with your heart and mind as well. Listen with your entire existence and consciousness. Listen to what is being spoken, listen to what is not being spoken, and understand it as well. Listen to the words, listen to the silence, listen to the wordless as well. One who understands the language of silence will also understand the language of words.

BASIS OF RELATIONSHIP

Relationships are very important in life. Relationships are made with love and trust. Doubt, suspicion, distrust create cracks and misunderstandings in relationships. Relationships are like plants- they have to be nurtured with love constantly- otherwise these relationships become weak. Handle and nurture relationships with love. Relationships are the identity of our personality. The stronger the relationships, the more comfortable, peaceful and joyful life will be.

AVOID CONDEMNATION

Condemnation is a negative thought, it reveals our jealousy. Reveals our hatred and ego. Then we complain, compare with others. Due to this we question our own abilities and capabilities. Condemnation is an escape, an escape from one's responsibility. Trying to make yourself look big by making others look small is meaningless and meaningless. Don't lower yourself in the eyes of your self. Will not be able to rise in the eyes of others.

DO AS YOU SAY

Words speak, but not more than actions. Let us not get stuck in mere words, let us not get entangled in illusion, let us do whatever we say. Otherwise we will not be able to become trustworthy. Neither in our own eyes, nor in the eyes of others. There is a great need for trust and confidence in the environment in life. We have to be united in mind, words and actions. We have to work as a united force. Our words and actions should be the same.

ENHANCE PERSONALITY

The behavior of the other person is negative, not good. As we understand it, he is delivering the hard ball. But we have to bat well, we have to be worthy. We should show gratitude to the other person. That it is playing an important role in the development of our personality and in improving our abilities. The person in front is showing hatred but he is becoming an instrument in awakening the feelings of compassion and kindness in us. We should use the bad behavior of others to bring out the best in ourselves.

THERE IS CHARM IN GIVING

We should love ourselves, respect ourselves, be confident and honest towards ourselves. We can share and give whatever we have. We should understand the other person's point of view. Everyone wants to get love, respect and trust, wants to be worthy of praise. We should neither think nor speak in vain. We just learn to give, sharing happiness and spreading love should become our nature.

BECOME CONFIDANT

People trust us, we owe it to them, we never break this trust. In today's world of lies, deceit and pretense, it is very important to have faith. Let us spread and share our faith in the society, in the family and in the world. The world needs trustworthy people. Trust is needed in relationships. We become such that people can trust us. If we have faith in ourselves, we will surely become trustworthy for others.

EXPECTATION IS TENSION

Expectation is sadness, disappointment, stress. It gives rise to anxiety, expectation reduces the happiness and joy of our life. The feeling of getting, the feeling of taking, the feeling of snatching, this feeling that I should get all this is tension. Immersion is necessary along with acquisition. By giving we become entitled to receive. Keep expectations to a minimum

WELCOME HAPPINESS

No one is interested in our sickness, disease or sorrow. If we are inconsolable, shedding tears, then we are alone. Let us not make sadness our habit. Let us welcome happiness, show curiosity in happiness. Let us not dump the garbage of sorrow in our neighborhood and around us. Let us sing praises of happiness and find ways to eradicate sorrow. Let sorrows be eradicated from the world, sorrows should be reduced, these should be our feelings. Let us not talk about disease, but about health, the aspiration should be for health and happiness

SPREAD HAPPINESS

Our words and our behavior should only be the cause of happiness for others and should never be the cause of sorrow. Don't keep expressing sorrow, don't spread sorrow. Cry in solitude, but do not share your sorrow, because 'whatever you share will come back', so be alert. We should sow only the seeds of happiness for ourselves, sow only the seeds of happiness, distribute only happiness. To get the sympathy of others, never be sad, be self-respecting. If you share happiness, happiness will increase. If you share your sorrow, your sorrow will increase.

EFFECT OF WORDS

We do not tie bonds through our words, we open them. May we shower only joy with our words. May our words be filled with good wishes, filled with good feelings. The words spoken by others are their own choice, they are the participants in it. We should not become dependent on the words of others. By understanding the meaning, subject and purpose of words, we should become free from empty words. Don't get lost in words, don't get confused. The negative words of others should not have a negative impact on us.

ELIGIBILITY REQUIRED

It is not possible to please everyone in life and be happy with everyone. Let us be happy, share happiness. Those who have eligibility and receptivity, those who want will be happy, otherwise they will not be. If someone wants to remain sad then who can make him happy? We can share, it is the responsibility of the other person to accept. If doors, windows, skylights are closed then light cannot reach there. No matter how bright it is outside! Must have eligibility.

SENSE OF APPRECIATION

We may see and hear the shortcomings of others, their mistakes and weaknesses, but do not think about them, do not give any place to the shortcomings in our mind. Because this will start a series of negative thoughts, over-thinking and stress. Our own energy levels will also diminish. So think well, have a sense of appreciation. This is beneficial for yourself as well as others. Let us send positive energy to others from our strong spiritual consciousness.

OUR BEHAVIOR

Our behavior should be easy, simple and free from deceit. There is no pretense, no deception, no deceit, no lies in behaviour. Needless complexity in relationships is painful. There should be love and truthfulness in our behaviour; we should become worthy of trust and confidence. This makes everyone happy and joyful. Our words should be such that we too become cool and others also feel cool. Our behavior towards others should always be cooperative.

PRAY

Have good wishes and prayers for all of us. Wish everyone's success, health, prosperity and progress wholeheartedly. We should never be jealous of the progress and prosperity of others. The prayer we pray for everyone gets fruitful in our own lives also. Therefore, pray with full consciousness and awareness. Never have any kind of ill will towards anyone, always have goodwill.

(4)

MIND

Disorder free mind, disorder free life - this is the music of life.

Victory over the mind is good luck, bad luck.

Our song is mind, it is love, it is love.

BEST FRIEND

Our mind is like a child. The mind is stubborn and does whatever is forbidden. He doesn't understand his own interests, he only has desires - if he doesn't agree, he gets sad and cries. Take care of your mind with love and patience, listen to him. Never do anything hastily or forcefully. Don't stop the mind, don't scold it. Praise him when he does good. If you do something wrong, explain it with love, explain it again and again, be patient. Cooperate and help in unleashing his power. Tell your mind that you are his best friend.

POWER OF DETERMINATION

Our every thought spreads far and wide in the form of a wave in the atmosphere. Faith in the mind, depth of feelings, determination and repetition convert our thoughts into reality. In this way very strong vibrations are created in nature. And nature accepts it. Our resolve manifests itself manifold in our lives. Energy is created through determination. With repeated resolution the energy becomes deeper and stronger. Resolve has immense power, it transforms life.

ORGANIZE THE MIND

Let us organize our subconscious mind in a new way. Change the negative attitude of mind into a positive state. Negative thoughts are not a stable thing, it is possible to drop them. We broke our superstitions and old beliefs. Because our thoughts and thoughts change according to our belief and faith; according to our thoughts, our thoughts and feelings change into words, and words into behavior and actions. So let us pay attention to our beliefs and beliefs. Break negativity through self-dialogue and self-suggestion.

MIND AND BODY

Our mind and body are connected to each other all the time. The body keeps changing into mind and the mind keeps changing into body. According to the thoughts and feelings of our mind, chemical reactions keep happening in the body, due to which the language and health of our body changes. If something happens to the body, the mind changes. So let us control our mind, be conscious of our thoughts and feelings and take care of our health. Good mind, good health are signs of a positive life.

NEGATIVE THOUGHTS

If the mind is negative, the thoughts will be negative. But we should not welcome such ideas, no one should take interest in them, no one should take interest in them. Don't give any strength to these thoughts. Don't trust them, doubt them. Question your mind on this topic. We will find that the mind has no answer, and even if a logical answer comes, then question that answer also. The mind will be speechless, then gradually the mind will agree. Be patient, don't rush.

TRAINING OF MIND

The mind is fickle by nature, the mind is a series of choices. But we can train our subconscious mind, give it self-suggestions, and gradually change the nature of the mind. With a calm mind, with full faith, in consciousness, we repeat again and again what we want to happen. Let us train our mind that no matter what the situation is, we have to remain positive.

THOUGHT CONTROL

We have to avoid the vicious circle of negative thoughts. The weakest point of any thought is its initial moment, be careful in the beginning itself, be alert. This is the time for change. Whatever idea you have, move on to a better idea. Understand the nature of the mind. The mind has to pay more attention to negative things. So be conscious, change your thoughts as soon as negative thoughts come, do this again and again.

DO NOT ACCEPT CONFLICT

We should be conscious of our thoughts and feelings, but should not go into conflict with them. Don't fight them, don't reject them, just accept them easily. Don't get worried, stay calm. Do not have a negative attitude. There is a negative invitation for the mind, understand the mind. Till date no one has been able to win the mind by fighting within the mind. First accept, then change peacefully, victory is ours.

GET WHATEVER YOU WANT

Everything is going well, everything will be fine, have such firm faith and belief in your mind. We are safe, the world is safe, all justice is here, peace is raining, first let us make our life like this. The world we really want is going to happen, there is no doubt, no doubt, such faith should be strong in the mind. First change your own world, the outside world will start changing. We should not become obstacles in our own desires, we should never think in the opposite direction, we should not doubt. Let us not become a red light on our own path, but a green light.

SAD HEART

A sad mind only gives sorrow. An unhappy mind thinks negatively, thinks wrongly, thinks excessively. We cannot trust a sad mind, a sad mind is unable to take right decisions. We should not let our mind remain in sorrow. May our hearts not keep crying. Through meditation, prayer, good company, by reading, writing or listening to something good, whatever way you can, bring yourself out of the sorrow of the mind. If any past experience is still a cause of sadness, then be forgiving towards yourself and everyone and open the knots of your mind. Happy mind, happy life.

THE DIFFICULTY IS IN THE MIND

The difficulty is not in life, not in relationships, it is in our mind, it is in the mind. Even if someone can remove the knots of the body, the knots of the mind have to be removed by oneself. When we think about others, our health becomes bad. Don't make life a burden. Whatever happens, it will be good, let us keep doing good. Whatever we welcome into our life, we get it. We are the first to hear all our abuses, we are the ones who get troubled.

KEEP THE FAITH

Even when difficulties and problems seem huge and there are no solutions in sight, do not lose hope. Have faith, be patient, some way will definitely appear. Our faith will employ our subconscious mind to think of solutions. Soon the mind will constantly suggest solutions to us. The power and energy of the universe will be with us. No difficulty can be bigger than this power. The answer will come from the subconscious mind. We will see the way.

SELF-DIALOGUE

Positive self-talk is the basis of a good and noble life. How we talk to ourselves is very important. Our self-talk plays an important role in our happiness and sorrow. Listen to the mind, understand the mind, make the mind understand. Self-dialogue is the best meditation. Tell yourself, he is our most trusted friend. It is a big thing to take the mind into confidence. Then he will definitely understand our understanding.

EXPRESS EMOTION

Whether your feelings are negative or positive, express them. Go to their root, find the reason. Mistake in understanding expressions creates a lot of misunderstanding and confusion in life. If there are some feelings inside, if they are expressed outside, then the feelings inside are repressed, the repressed feelings go deep into the subconscious mind. And cause many types of diseases and problems. Positive emotions are beneficial for everyone. Don't deprive yourself or the world of this.

USE YOUR MIND

The mind keeps insisting like a child. He keeps expressing his wishes and desires, and we run after him, get busy in fulfilling his wishes and desires. The mind is the driver of all the senses, so first control the mind. The mind gets controlled during meditation, but meditation cannot be done forcibly. Do some homework first. Let the mind work as per its interest, work with excellent and meaningful expression. So that the thoughts are reduced and an environment can be created to enter into meditation.

LOSERS OF THE MIND

The biggest problem is to consider the problem as a problem. What is the problem? Any challenge, any possibility – face them, welcome them. With positive energy, turn the problem into a molehill and not a mountain. Our perspective is decisive. The mind has the art of making the small big and the big small. Use this art. Consider challenge as a game and play has its own joy. There is no competition here. Just don't lose, just win. Losers of the mind lose, winners of the mind win.

MIND IS MANTRA

Mind is mantra, mind is mantra. The mind repeats, this is its art, process, power. We get attracted to what we see and hear again and again. Repetition of an idea in the mind takes the form of reality. If the mantra has to be changed then it has to be broken with the opposite mantra. The current idea should be more powerful than the previous idea. Break the idea of illness with the idea of getting health. Focus on the right. Don't use negative words, they are more powerful.

REDUCE STRESS

Stress is the lack of balance in the energy and state of the body and mind, ignorance of the order and truth within us, the gap between our expectations and reality. Tension is uncomfortable, sadness is. The world cannot work as we think all the time. Make the mind your friend, understand it. Take help of meditation, do some thinking. The more the mind is in our favor, the less will be the stress.

GUARDING THOUGHTS

Every thought of ours is a wave, and every wave has its own special vibration. The state of mind is formed according to the thoughts. Thoughts take the form of words. Every word also has its own power, energy, vibration. Different vibration waves have different effects on each of our cells. This is an invisible power, but very powerful. Our thoughts and emotions have a deep impact on our lives. Let us handle it at the level of thinking only.

BALANCE OF MIND

Maintaining a state of equanimity in happiness and sorrow, keeping the lamp of confidence and hope lit, is balance of mind. The situation is not always the same. Be it favorable or unfavorable, nothing is going to last, everything has to come and go. Therefore, remain happy and positive in every situation. Don't cling to favorable circumstances, don't be careless. Don't get lost in adversity, don't get disheartened. Have to maintain a positive attitude and strong willpower.

FEELING OF HAPPINESS AND SADNESS

We are sad because of ourselves, and we are happy because of ourselves. The feeling of happiness and sorrow is in our thinking. Let us refine our own values, clean our viewpoint. It is because of our negative thinking as a reaction that we become sad and in pain. Do not associate your mind with those whose mental state is weak and who have negative attitudes.

STATE OF MIND

We should not let circumstances dominate our state of mind. Don't let circumstances control your state of mind. Whatever may be the situation, stability of mind should be maintained. We find sorrow even in good things, then why can't we find goodness and happiness in evil and negativity? After the dark night comes a bright day. Even if the situation is adverse, we can keep our mind in a favorable state, it is just a matter of changing our perspective.

RELAXATION OF MIND

Relaxation of mind is very important. So that we can do our work feeling light and fresh, let us do our work by being detached and unattached. Be aware and do action without reaction, the mind will get relaxation. Let us perform holy and wise actions. If we simply exist and desire nothing, the mind will find deep relaxation.

UNDERSTAND THE MIND

The mind is ours, we are not the mind, always remember this. It is our job to understand and explain the mind. Control of mind should be in our hands. It is our responsibility to give positive thoughts to the mind. We should repeat all those things again and again with great love and patience that we want to make the mind the way we want. Make your mind believe. Tell your mind only what you really want to see in reality. The mind can be controlled only by love.

REMAIN NEUTRAL

It is the nature of the mind that those things which we try to stop and suppress, they necessarily come before us in life. So whatever we don't want in life, don't stop it, don't stop it, accept it, face it but don't react, don't go into conflict, don't even welcome it, it will automatically go away slowly. We should not show any interest or enthusiasm in those things. Remain equanimous, remain neutral. Focus all our attention on what we want to achieve in life.

SPEECH AND MIND

Our speech gets affected by the overthinking of the fickle mind, the racing of the mind, the murmuring of the mind. We destroy the meaning. Our mind keeps getting entangled in useless, unrestrained and false arguments. We can reduce the restlessness of our mind through meditation. Then it becomes easier to express in words what is in the mind. We should not speak whatever we are asked to say, we should speak only what we want to speak. Speech should come from the heart. Our mind should remain in our speech, that is, when we speak, our mind speaks only then.

AS YOU THINK, SO IS THE WORLD

Whatever our mind thinks, we become like that, our world becomes like that. We are the fruit of our own thinking. Our thoughts are us. If we think that we are happy and will remain happy then no power in the world can make us sad. If we think that we will lose, we are bound to lose. If we talk about courage, there will be courage

BELIEF-DISBELIEF

Belief and disbelief both are special powers and energies of the mind. These have miraculous powers. We can do it, this is faith. We can't believe it, disbelieve it. Both work equally in themselves. Be sure to connect faith with your resolution. Keep distance from mistrust. Otherwise disbelief will destroy our faith. Let us believe in our faith. Let creation happen, do not talk about destruction. Life is ours, we decide our own value.

OUR WORLD

Our likes and dislikes, desires, interests, our focus, our attention, thoughts, views, this is our world. Whatever we want to happen, will happen. But the things that we fear and wish should not happen are also a part of our world. Whatever positive or negative thoughts we have, that is who we are. The world is as we are. The world is an echo. That is why despite living in the same world, everyone's world is different.

BECOME MASTER OF MIND

When someone laughs, satirizes or insults our shortcomings and weaknesses, do not get angry, do not curse yourself, smile within yourself, smile at yourself. By getting angry, the power of the other person increases, if we don't, our power will increase. It is only when we feel insulted that someone else is able to insult us. If we are determined to win, no one can defeat us. The losers of the mind lose, the winners of the mind win. We became masters of our minds. If we are determined, our mind will follow us.

MIND IS A MIRROR

A calm mind is like a mirror, in it we are able to see our truth clearly. A calm mind is concentrated, pure and stress free. The more peace, the more relaxation. Rest is peace. When relaxed, the mind becomes sharp, alert and happy. A calm mind is happy and satisfied. In peace and silence, we can taste the drizzle of joy that is falling within us every moment, that inner glory.

WHATEVER YOU WANT WILL HAPPEN

Focus all our attention on what we want in life. We should not pay attention to those things which we do not want to happen in life. We want health, let's talk about health only. We should invest all our energy, time and power in those things which we want in life. Let us talk about those whom we like. Think what is good. If you think otherwise, there will be adverse results in life. Because whatever we think, whatever we believe appears before us in the form of reality.

(5)

Truth – Dedication - Achievement

It is what it is – this is the truth. Meditation is an inner journey. It is the achievement of the self.

Be aware of your senses. Don't beg from the world market,
Pass through the market, see, but remain untouched,
Markets should not create greed and desire within us.

CONSCIOUSNESS AWAKENS

Mechanics are a hindrance in realizing the truth. Civilization is making man mechanical. Man is competing with the machine. Mechanical discipline, which is devoid of feeling, keeps moving us away from sensitivity. Inertia is taking us away from ourselves. Mechanical habit suppresses consciousness. We have to work with our consciousness and sensitivity. Work has to be done knowingly, not unknowingly. Our work should not create inertia in us, it should awaken the light of consciousness.

TRUTH IS IN ITSELF

Truth is not somewhere outside, it is within us. We should know this through feeling and experience. Our awareness and selfless feelings become the reason for the truth to become available. Search yourself, dig yourself - come to yourself. No reaction, no evaluation, just be an observer, do self-observation. Man is engrossed in others, he is afraid of being alone. But there is no truth in the crowd. The truth is that whatever is within oneself can be found only there, not anywhere else.

SEARCH FOR TRUTH

Freedom is the first condition in the search for truth. A slavery imposed by others on us. A slavery we impose upon ourselves. We are imprisoned in our own beliefs and assumptions. We have tied ourselves in bonds. This belief is a step towards truth. All our pain and sorrow bear our signature. Recognize them, only in this recognition we become easy, simple and independent. We find an innocent mind free from complications, which is essential in the search for truth.

FEELING OF LIBERATION

When there is a confluence of knowledge and meditation in life, then we understand the meaning of life, the essence of life. Then we do not live by fear, we do not live by dying. We live a life of faith and devotion. The more auspicious our feelings are, the more fearless we will be. Truth and beauty will be revealed in life. Everything is impermanent – this realization should always remain. There is a shadow of fear in life due to lies and pretense. If we live in truth, we will realize salvation.

INNER JOURNEY

The treasure of love, peace and happiness lies within us, not anywhere outside, reveal them. So the search should be done within, not outside. Become a less active participant in the outside hustle and bustle. This also helps in reducing the inner voice and makes the inner journey possible, so that one can live in one's own nature. This is where the treasure will be found, this is also where there is freedom from vices. When we go away from ourselves, we suffer from disorders. Therefore, keep distance from those who distance us from ourselves, pay attention to company.

MEDITATION- UNDISTURBED MIND

Meditation is a delicate thing, it cannot be forced. There is no organization for this. Sometimes it happens spontaneously in a quiet moment. Just relax yourself, be relaxed, don't get anxious. We should leave ourselves open and free, not tied. Meditation is the art of removing the curtain of thoughts between us and the world. It is a flower, that's all - it is not a matter of whether it is beautiful or ugly. Meditation is the undisturbed mind, the ascent of consciousness.

MEDITATION AND PRAYER

Life becomes better only through meditation and prayer. Meditation and prayer are the blessings of life. There is peace, joy, relaxation. There is nothing to be gained in prayer. Have a feeling of gratitude for what you have received, be grateful, be filled with thanks. Meditation is to empty oneself, to become void. Don't have to hold on to anything, don't have to get stuck anywhere. We have to reveal ourselves so that the seed can become a tree. What was unrevealed became visible.

ATTENTION

We all have experience with meditation. Without meditation, even small work in life cannot be accomplished. Meditation is a lifestyle. This is easy, natural. Every action in life has to be done with awareness, awareness is meditation. Becoming one with mind, words and actions is a form of meditation. Meditation is the best medium for improvement and change in life. We should live in awareness, not in unconsciousness. Be conscious, meditation will happen spontaneously. Meditation is the ultimate journey, the achievement of the self.

SHINE IN YOUR NATURE

In meditation, one has to face the subject with a calm mind, with neutrality, with equanimity, with awareness. Know the subject from its roots, know it completely, the solution is certain. We can remove the impurities and disorders of the mind from life through meditation, so that we can shine in our nature. Meditation brings the mind under control. Meditation reduces conflict, unrest, stress in life and gives freedom from overthinking and negative thinking.

MEDITATION-LIVING IN THE PRESENT

Life is in the present moment only, meditation teaches us to be in the present, to live in the present. Focus on your breathing, focus on your thoughts, focus on sensations. Only observation and a sense of neutrality – this is what has to be learned. Let us remain alert every moment, so that we can handle the present moment. This is sadhana. As long as we are where we are, let us do whatever we are doing - otherwise we will not go astray. Maintain stability of mind, only a stable mind can become calm.

LIFE OF CONSCIOUSNESS

We should remain conscious in our thinking, speech, behavior and every action. Our sleeping, walking, getting up, sitting, eating, reading, writing, listening, all our activities should be done judiciously and consciously. This is meditation – meditation is not just a matter of some time. Life should be conscious, an awakened life – this is religion, this is meditation. Be aware of your anger and also be aware of your forgiveness. Consciousness keeps the meaningful in life and discards the meaningless.

SENSE OF SEPARATENESS

We are not thoughts, we are different, thoughts are different. The process of meditation is the realization of separation with thoughts. This is both science and art. Whatever we are awake and aware of, it disappears. The fear of whomever you fear will enter your mind. No one can win by fighting with the mind. We do not fight with ideas, fighting gives strength to ideas. "I am not darkness, I am the sun." No matter how close or strong the darkness is, I cannot be afraid of it.

WITNESSING ATTITUDE

Meditation establishes us in the state of observer, witnessing. Teaches the lesson of neutrality and equality in life, takes one into silence. In meditation there is no noise, no choice, no struggle, there is a feeling of acceptance, no neglect, no complaint, there is a feeling of thanks, gratitude. Meditation is a feeling of forgiveness, wishing well for everyone. Meditation makes us light, comfortable and refreshed. Meditation increases willpower. In meditation we read the lesson of reactive lifestyle.

AWAKENING IS GOOD

Meditation breaks the mind and brings awakening. Continuity of meditation leads to higher consciousness. Whatever we do, we should be aware of it, not do it unknowingly. Whatever happens unknowingly, in the will, is inauspicious. Unknowingly, under the influence of emotions, under the influence of some belief or belief, we start getting carried away by attachment or hatred. Taking steps towards awakening through meditation is auspicious and auspicious in our life.

BECOME ZERO

Be an investigator, be curious, observe yourself so that you come to your senses and remain conscious. If consciousness remains, beliefs and superstitions will be broken. The path to self will be easy. Let the experiencer come into the experience. Become empty from inside, become zero. Whatever is negative has to be left. Don't hold on to what is positive, because what is ours is ours in any case. Aim to become empty, zero, become light, so that the consciousness can achieve upward movement.

WORDS BECOME NECTAR

When we understand the mystery of life, step on the path of truth and our mind starts following us, our words start becoming loving, effective and full of joy. We can understand the importance of pronunciation, then our words can transform enmity into love, defeat into victory. Words can be formed like cool shade, treatment, medicine. May our words become nectar, may we move forward in a positive direction, bind everyone in the bond of love and spread happiness in everyone's life.

LUCK AND EFFORT

We write our destiny by making efforts every moment and to make our destiny come true then efforts become necessary. If our thinking is correct, our efforts are good, our mind is positive, then whatever our fate may be, we make it auspicious. We are unique, special, special. We can learn good from evil also. We can convert evil into good. Our destiny is our efforts.

WRITE YOUR DESTINY

Every morning we make a code for the day. Some rules, some conduct, behavior, small goals, peace of mind, happiness etc. - how are we going to work on these. Every day let us decide our scope, method, and complete it. The way we live from moment to moment, our lifestyle, decides our destiny. We are creating our destiny by doing every action. So destiny didn't ask for it, it didn't make it, I don't know how to write it myself. Staying positive in the present is the only way to change your destiny.

AVOID 'EXTREME'

We should not be so fond of anyone that we cannot live without him, and we should not hate anyone so much that we cannot live with his presence. 'Excess' of everything is bad. 'Extreme' only brings sorrow, trouble and difficulty in life. Too closeness and too much distance create rift in relationships also. A distance, a thin curtain is necessary. In the laws of nature, in the laws of law, everything is coordinated, in harmony, there is nothing in 'excess

DON'T LIVE IN TEMPTATION

Do not live in attachment, those who live in attachment become dependent and dependent in life. In the name of affection, in the name of love – don't get stuck in attachment. Do not harm yourself or your loved ones. People, things and events will come and go in life. Do not create attachment to them, do not identify with them. Watch them coming and going, keep some distance. Let us pray that everyone should be free from attachment, that no one should be dependent on anyone, that all the people of the world should become self-reliant. May we be free from the attachment of our thoughts, vices and supports. Make liberation the goal, so that attachment decreases.

WHAT KIND OF EGO

We are in ego. What is our own? Does breathing happen as per our wish? Does it stop? Is meeting and separation in our hands? The loss of youth and the coming of old age, do we decide? Position, property, body, beauty, youth, do we have the right, dominance, control over these? We do not want to understand the impermanence of life. So we do not live a life of truth. Live a life of lies and pretense. Then we are worried about why there is sorrow in life? Contemplate, contemplate.

KNOW THE ANGER

Anger is momentary madness, anger is the end of the self in itself. We must face anger, do not suppress anger, suppressing anger is not right, we have to make eye contact with anger. Find the reason for anger, rejoice in its roots, understand that facing anger weakens it. Gradually diminishes, then ends. Keep observing. Speak the truth to yourself, do not deceive yourself. Don't cheat, be honest, the results will be surprising.

IDENTITY IS SORROW

Pain comes and goes on the body, we identify ourselves with this pain. This is the grip, the sorrow, the obstacle. On the surface of the mind, thoughts and feelings come and go like clouds, we go together with them. As if we are the mind. 'We are neither a body nor a mind, things come and go on me, but I am different from them, separate, untouched.' The room is filled with darkness, I have become a little dark. There is no victory in fighting with the mind and body, there is victory in seeing, knowing and understanding them.

BREAK UNCONSCIOUSNESS

Our desires create us. Lust is the rope, the bond, this is the sorrow. We are the accumulation of our own desires. We have created ourselves. Stupor, sleep, unconsciousness, is deep, it has to be broken continuously. Laziness will lead you astray and will lead to waste. But let us try holistically and single-mindedly. The unconsciousness will break, consciousness will come, alertness will come. We have to light the lamp within ourselves - the rules of the world are neutral. If we follow the right path, we will get support.

FEAR FREE LIFE

Considering yourself one with the body and mind, this identification is fear. Do not escape from fear, do not run away, do not be afraid. Face it, look into its eyes. There is something in our inner being which has no death, become its seeker, taste it. Meditate on fear. If you feel afraid, sit quietly and look at the fear, observe it. Do not be afraid of fear, fear will not eliminate it. This task will be possible only by being fearless.

RECOGNIZE THE OPPORTUNITY

Opportunity knocks at our door again and again. We must recognize this opportunity. We must not waste it. This is a chance to improve and refine ourselves. Recognizing this opportunity requires a calm and steady mind, the power of understanding, the experience of spiritual practice, and awareness. We must understand things holistically. Pain itself becomes medicine; darkness brings light, so be patient. Don't worry, don't stress, and remain positive so that the opportunity is not lost.

STAY STRESS FREE

Today, stress is increasing in life. Instead of appearing as what we are, we are engaged in trying to appear as something else. We want to be what we are not. Stress is natural. We are not machines, mechanicalness cannot be our style. We should become sensitive. Outside there is anger, ego - inside there is fear and helplessness. This is stress. Outside there is lie, inside there is repression - this is stress. Inside there is suppressed guilt, we cannot forgive the mistakes of others, there is a feeling of revenge. We should become strong, face the truth and live a stress-free life.

SORROW IS A FRIEND

Consider sorrow as your friend, a beneficial friend. We learn great lessons from sorrow. Most of our experiences are gained from sorrow. Sorrow becomes the reason for the search for truth. In sorrow we remember God. If there is sorrow, we search for happiness. Sorrow is the script of happiness. If there is sorrow, accept it, do not deny it, face the sorrow - the sorrow will reduce. Sorrow brings us closer to ourselves. In happiness we forget ourselves.

ACCOMPLISHMENT THROUGH RESOLUTION

Creation and success are possible through resolve. Resolutions are what transform reality. Teach the mind a new language of resolve. Bring the mind out of old beliefs and superstitions. Have a deep faith that whatever you want will happen. Establish this faith deep within your mind, repeat it, and then become an effortful person so that your desire can become reality. Wake up in the morning with resolve and sleep at night with resolve. This is meditation. Meditation is the process of transforming thoughts into reality.

GURU'S ARRIVAL

When a thirst for truth awakens in life, a Guru comes. We receive guidance from the Guru to understand our true face, our inner face, and how to see the face where truth resides. Each word of the Guru will shatter our beliefs and superstitions. Virtues will manifest, and we will become immensely fortunate. Let this be our prayer: let us live life consciously. Sow the seeds of faith, do not doubt. You will reap miraculous results.

SELF-CONTROL

Life is about minimizing suffering, not suppressing it. Give direction to your tears. Purify and purify yourself through your own tears. Don't keep crying for others. Don't be hasty in forming opinions about anyone. Don't react hastily to any event or situation. Understand the entire subject in the light of knowledge. We must correctly understand the nature, habits, and perspectives of our mind. Only then is self-control possible.

JOURNEY OF SELF REALIZATION

To make the mind happy, one should not just keep pleasing the senses unnecessarily. Have control over the mind. Whatever the mind believes, that starts happening. Understand the power of the mind. Handle the cycle of excitement and disappointment in the mind. We should give a big goal to life. Give the mind a big task. For this, it will be of great help in bringing the mind out of its negative grip, attachment, and the mind's stuckness and wandering. The journey of self-realization will begin.

INNER VOICE

People will say many things in life; it's their job to say things. The intellect will test itself, and arguments will abound. The mind will play many tricks, drawing us into conflict and conflict. But we must listen to the voice of our heart, our inner self. The voice within us is a reflection of our divine power and energy. Our inner self is connected to the universe. We must develop the ability to listen and understand the voice of our inner self.

TRUTH OF THE MOMENT

Death in a moment, life in a moment. Every moment is birth, every moment is death. We should live and feel each moment. Welcome and respect each moment. We should also bid farewell to each moment with love. Inhaled in a moment, exhaled in a moment. Trying to capture moments is futile. Sunshine in a moment, shade in a moment, accident in a moment, miracle in a moment. Know the changeability and impermanence of life.
Understand the truth of birth and death.

ATTACHMENT AND DETACHMENT

Attachment and detachment are not related to things, not to the outside. They are related to our thoughts, emotions, and the world within us. What we have and how much we have is not important. What matters is how attached we are to them, how detached we are. This is a matter of contemplation and understanding. The world should not reside in our minds. The world's presence in the mind itself is attachment, bondage. We should live and bloom like a lotus.

AUSPICIOUS FEELING, AUSPICIOUS MOMENT

When we live consciously and with awareness, and there is purity in the mind, then the mind remains in auspicious feelings. It remains full of enthusiasm and excitement, thoughts become meaningful and noble. This is the auspicious moment, the auspicious moment. Every moment in life is an obstacle, every moment is suitable. Auspicious feeling means, the appropriate moment. Do not let it go, use it. If for some reason the feeling is inauspicious, then that moment is not appropriate. Stop, change the feeling. Changing the feeling is in our hands, just be alert.

KHOLE MIND KNOT

The accumulated negative things and impulses of the past keep bothering us even today, knowingly or unknowingly, from time to time. We have tied knots in our minds, only we can untie them. We can free ourselves from the guilt of the past. Make forgiveness our basis. Forgive yourself first. Forgive everyone, forgive everyone – develop such a feeling. The feeling of forgiveness is not a favor to anyone, it is a favor to ourselves. Forgiveness makes us pure, clean. It takes away our burdens, frees us from bondage.

BE RECEPTIVE

When we are calm and relaxed, we become more receptive. From nature and the universe, we receive messages, guidance, opportunities, and even coincidences. But if we are not receptive, we often fail to understand them. Grace is pouring down, but we become worthy of it only when we are receptive. There are also some internal messages; to hear them, the inner noise must be quieted.

CREATION BY DETERMINATION

Whether the goal is small or big, to accomplish it, one needs strong will power and determination. One needs 100% perseverance. Just like water turns into steam at 100 degrees. If you want to do anything, first make a resolution, repeat it in your mind with full consciousness again and again. Think, say – this will definitely happen and then make efforts to make the resolution a reality. Don't get entangled in options, they become a burden in life. Don't wander here and there, keep your eyes on the goal only. As is the resolution, so is the creation.

WHICH IS HUNDRED

Know what is, as it is, not otherwise. Whatever it is, it is. Regardless of the person or situation. Truth exists in its entirety, not in its incompleteness. It's essential to examine it from every perspective; it's impossible to reach the truth from a single perspective, with incomplete information. Don't impose your own feelings, your own evaluations, your own reactions—whatever they are—on the facts. See and understand them as they are. Maintain an unbiased view, a detachment.

LIFE IS A BLESSING

Life is a divine blessing, a gift. Life is a prasad. The purity, beauty, and innocence of life must be preserved in every situation. We must become trees. Our sheets must not remain as they are. We must advance the journey of life from the mind to the heart. We must make life useful. We must open the doors of our inner self, delve into the depths of our hearts. The doors to infinite possibilities will open. We will be able to express divine qualities.

SELF DISCIPLINE

We should teach ourselves the lesson of discipline; it will be very effective and meaningful. If we pretend to be disciplined or adopt it out of fear or influence of others, then discipline will give us a feeling of subjugation. We should make our own law, our constitution. Follow it and become independent. We should become independent ourselves and participate in making others independent too. If we are unable to discipline ourselves, then someone else will discipline us, and we will become dependent.

STAY INSIDE, LIVE OUTSIDE

There is contradiction in life. Action and inaction, motion and stillness, impermanence and eternity. We have to establish harmony in the opposition, bring balance. Motion and stillness are two sides of the same coin. Life is in motion, we are in motion, but within us there is stability; this is harmony. Maintaining the awareness of eternity amidst all change is life's balance, awareness. Inside, we should be situated in ourselves. All the activities of life should continue outside. Understand this truth deeply. Live within, live without.

ALWAYS BE HAPPY

Whenever pain, sorrow or trouble comes in life, do not say that 'I am sad', 'I am troubled'. We are not the body, nor the mind, we are the conscious observer, the conscious witness, we are not sad, yes, sorrow has come in life now. It will pass, it was bound to come in the journey, the path is like this. We should remain in our nature, remember ourselves and be happy. We should believe this in our mind. We should remain happy even in difficulties because happiness brings happiness and sorrow brings sorrow.

UNDERSTAND FEELINGS

We are unable to understand our own emotions properly; our emotions act like fog, like clouds. That is why we should understand emotions with intelligence and discretion. Do not deny emotions, do not hide them, do not start saying good or bad, do not suppress them, face them, understand them. Someone said something, I felt bad, this feeling of bad is not anyone else's fault, it is my reaction. It is my own emotional state, I am responsible for it. With our intelligence, we can give our emotions a meaningful, positive direction.

LIFE OF HARMONY

Nature is in perfect harmony, in a rhythm. We should remain in harmony, live harmoniously. There is a synchronization between the earth's magnetic force and our spine; this is the source of energy and life force. Nature is guiding every living being towards harmony. This signal will always be positive; negative thoughts cannot be a signal. We should understand the signals. Stress, doubt, and distrust are obstacles; keep distance from them. Stay calm and relaxed.

LIKES AND DISLIKES

We want what we like—we are happy with it. If we get what we dislike, we become unhappy. But our likes can change at any time. And it's not necessary that what we like is in our best interest. Likes and dislikes are superficial things; don't get entangled in them. Let them go; nothing will last. Live with aspirit of acceptance. We will surely get what is ours. "Want," "don't want"—that is sorrow

ASEEM'S JOURNEY

Let us not see ourselves as bodies, as individuals. We are infinite consciousness. We are not limited; only a person living in a body can think limitedly. Let us compete with ourselves, not with others, and make ourselves better than ourselves. Let us allow divine qualities to manifest in our lives. Our potential is limitless. Divine qualities will be able to take us on a journey to the infinite. We must move forward.

RULE OF LAW

The thought, "I shouldn't have problems," is the problem itself. Problems will come and go, according to the law of nature. The problem isn't ours; we simply need to find a solution—that's our karma. If we find a solution, we will be rewarded with love, peace, and joy, according to the law of nature. How we solve the problem is crucial. Look at the problem in parts, not as a whole; we are one. Then victory is certain.

MANNERS WITH MEANS

Resources and facilities are essential in life. Resources provide civilization, and values create culture. Resources can provide a vehicle, but it is values that determine life's direction. Until we understand the meaning and essence of life, the secrets of joy and sorrow, we cannot successfully face adversity. To prevent accidents in life, the vehicle of life requires the culture of restraint along with resources.

HAPPINESS IS THE PATH AND THE DESTINATION TOO

We shouldn't approach our tasks as a burden, a disappointment, or a compulsion. We should do them consciously, with full energy, and happily. Work done in desperation or compulsion cannot bring us happiness. Working happily is the true way to be happy. This is both the path and the destination; happiness is present in every moment. Develop interest in your work, understand its bright side, and work happily.

TIME MANAGEMENT

Time is precious; life is all about time. Use it meaningfully. Manage your time. Devote maximum and quality time to important and auspicious tasks. Don't postpone tasks until tomorrow. Time is here, right now, and right now. We only have one moment at a time. Determine precisely how much time to devote to each task, when to devote it, and how to devote it. Understand the importance of time.

MIND IS MIRROR

If the mind is calm and pure, life becomes a philosophy, not a display. Life becomes service, a pilgrimage. When the mind is calm, it becomes a mirror; we can see our truth in it. It will be clearly visible. Peace lies in the stillness of mind; peace cannot be found anywhere else. A restless mind spreads sorrow. Do not increase anyone's sorrow; there is already a lot of sorrow. Peace is not something to be asked for; peace can only be attained through inner development.

EMBRACE FORGIVENESS

The combined effects of our thoughts, emotions, impulses, and expressions impact the world. We are responsible for the world as it is today. Taking this responsibility, let's become apologists. First, we must apologize to ourselves. Let's become awakened individuals. Cleanse our inner selves, and the outside will be cleansed. Wash away the past with the waters of forgiveness Forgive everyone, forgive everyone. With this attitude, let's work with fresh, new ideas.

ENJOY THE TASTE OF EQUALITY.

In happiness or sorrow, in praise or criticism, those who are not controlled by their desires, have a sense of equality, remain neutral, the splendor of peace and joy resides in their life. By having equality in our mind, we can become free from the ill effects of favorable and unfavorable circumstances that may occur in our life. In equality, we do not get stuck in happiness, nor do we wander in sorrow. In a life that changes every moment, equality is the path and also the destination. Let us enjoy equality and achieve the benefit of ourselves and everyone

FRIENDSHIP IS MAKEUP

I have no enmity with anyone, I am friends with everyone, such is the feeling of friendship. There is no hatred in this feeling. Love for all and well-being for all is the basis of friendship. May a source of compassion flow in our hearts for those who are sad, troubled, and in trouble. May the spirit of service and charity remain. May everyone be happy and joyful, such auspicious feelings prevail. May such a yearning arise in the heart for the well-being of all living beings.

PASSION AND HATRED

Love and hatred are the seeds of action, they arise from attachment. Love is attraction, attachment. Hatred is repulsion, opposition. Catch the action from the seed, start from the beginning. The wave of a small thought will take the form of reality tomorrow. Before action, wake up to the thought itself, because the thought means that half the work is done. The seed has fallen into the ground, the real thing has happened. We are living in a sleepy state. We want to wander, that is why we are wandering. Only through our decision can the suffering end and it will definitely end.

PURIFICATION OF FEELINGS

If the heart is calm, simple and pure, then the emotions become pure. The mind becomes free from anger and ill will. Purity in emotions is helpful in self-interest and welfare of others. Whatever the situation, the emotions of the mind should not be spoiled. We are not harmed by someone doing bad to us or by someone doing bad to us. When we start thinking bad and spoil our emotions, only then can we suffer loss. Avoid ill will, it is painful. We should maintain purity in our emotions.

MIRACLE IN FORGIVENESS

Forgiveness means protecting oneself and untangling one's own knots. Forgiveness creates a loving relationship with oneself and also fosters loving bonds with others. Forgiveness is the foundation of friendship and compassion. So, if we cleanse ourselves with forgiveness, change will begin outside. Everyone is our own, no one is a stranger. Forgiveness is worship, not utterance of the lips. Forgiveness is the harvest of the heart, compassion of the mind, and the practice of life.

(6)

Love Bliss Silence

The true recognition of oneself is liberation, this is bliss.

Silence is a journey to nothingness.

There is a drizzle of love and joy within us every moment, let us become calm and silent

OF EMPTINESS AND

When we are in prayer, meditation, and awareness, silence begins to occur. We become calm and empty, like a blank sheet of paper. God signs on a blank sheet of paper. In silence, ego dissolves, and a sense of surrender arises. We are able to hear the voice of our inner self. As we become aware of our ignorance, the inner journey begins. The turmoil and noise of the mind diminish, and inner awareness awakens.

FOUNTAIN OF LOVE

The purity and sanctity of the inner world is the foundation for the origin of love in the heart. Self-love and self-respect are crucial. This is also the foundation of universal love. The love we have for all creation, for all living beings, gives birth to an inner music within our lives. Our entire lives then become music. Love is the adornment of life, its beauty. An endless fountain of divine love flows within us; let us become drenched in it.

LOVE BECOMES PRAYER

Unconditional and selfless love is the pure expression of our consciousness, a prayer. Such love is not for a particular person, but for every living being, for every particle of nature. Love is not a choice; it is the spontaneity of life. Love is the feeling of acceptance, of giving. Here, one gives and receives. Goodness, well-wishes, and auspiciousness automatically become the call of the heart. A drizzle of love pours within us every moment; let us savor this inner glory.

LOVE YOURSELF

Everyone is searching for love, and the fountain of love flows uninterruptedly within us. Upon recognizing ourselves, we begin to love ourselves. Understand the law of love: love is not a choice; it is unconditional and universal. Self-love means universal love, love for all, love everywhere. Taste, desire, and lust cannot diminish our loneliness. Indulging in construction, creation, and music can bring a temporary sense of liberation. But fulfillment lies in meditation and spiritual practice.

CELEBRATION

Unconditional love infuses silence into life. Love deepens in silence. Life begins to reek of truth and honesty. Honesty makes life simple and easy. Zeal and enthusiasm for truth begin to overflow automatically. Happiness and smile in life should be such that it feels like a flute is playing, and speaking should feel like flowers are falling. Then your very existence, your presence, begins to shower peace and give solace. An atmosphere of joy—the message of love from spoken silence. Life becomes a celebration—a celebration of joy.

EXPRESSION OF LOVE

Love is expressed throughout nature. There is no greater experience or knowledge than love. The absence of love in life is the greatest ignorance, illiteracy, and poverty. In the absence of love, life becomes devoid of enthusiasm and excitement. Life becomes a place of wandering and fear. When ego falls, love blossoms. Let love germinate in the heart. Love is the name of a blissful life. One who reads two and a half letters of love becomes a scholar.

SILENT MEDITATION

Our inner self has no language. Words don't reach us, but silence—the wordless. Silence is the language of existence, the realization of our own existence. We exist, we are happy, we are blissful. We feel grace, nothingness. No emotions, no thoughts, just the awareness of our own existence. Silence is energy, a practice, the art of coming closer to ourselves. If we yearn to know ourselves, silence automatically enters our lives.

POWER OF SILENCE

Only the realization of the truth of "Who am I?" will introduce us to silence. Silence brings the blessings of love, joy, and peace into life. Then the mind becomes a flower. Peace comes into life, and then bowing down becomes natural. Then, no matter the situation, the mind does not become restless or anxious; it remains stable and unperturbed. Energy and power develop in silence, and decision-making becomes sharp. Truth is revealed only in silence.

WORDS OF SILENCE

It is only in the emptiness and silence of the mind that one encounters oneself. Words are limited, unable to express the truth. Let there be silence in the depths of the heart. Let the mind's futile movements, its restlessness, its rush, diminish. So that in silence we can feel the divinity and the supernaturalness of life. We can establish ourselves at the center of ourselves, and become situated in ourselves. Then the words uttered from the heart will be like nectar. They will make life joyful and fragrant.

SILENCE AND SMILE

Truth infuses love and silence into life. Silence is a protective shield, a safety for life. A smile welcomes us into life. It makes us spontaneous, prosperous, and innocent. It creates a radiance, vigor, and magnetic attraction within us. Silence is to be renewed, to be refreshed. Silence is the most powerful voice. Silence says everything that words cannot.

LANGUAGE OF SILENCE

The entire nature is enjoying silence. We too should enjoy silence, understand the language of silence, and become receptive. We should not get entangled in our likes and dislikes; we should be sensitive to everything. Whatever nature has given us, we should not make it a cause of sorrow in our lives. Use it meaningfully, and life will become blessed. We should continuously hone our intellect and discretion. Do the right thing at the right time, in the right way. Nature will always make itself available to us. Everything will prove to be a blessing for us.

REMAIN SILENT

Life expands from within to the outside, not from the outside to the inside. Life's roots lie within. We must work on these roots. Discover them, know them, and understand them. Enter into meditation, cultivate silence. Achieve emptiness, and let the truth be revealed. Silence transforms us into a calm, clear mirror. In it, we see our own truth. Then it becomes a song. The silence will deepen. The attainment of life's deepest truth, the realization of the highest goal, will become possible.

TRANSFORMATION INTO SILENCE

Silence is nothingness, peace, and bliss. Become silent not just with words, but with the mind. The mind's wanderings should subside, thoughts should diminish. Silence is the purity and stability of the mind. In silence, the mind undergoes a radical transformation, a transformation. Everything important in life happens in silence. All of nature is giving the message of silence. Only silence, not words, can express the truth. May I become silent not just with words, but with the mind.

SEARCH FOR HAPPINESS

Joy and happiness follow love. When we enjoy being happy, living in love, then why despair and disappointment in life? Don't be overwhelmed by sorrow and pain; it's natural. Sorrow is the foundation of happiness. If there is sorrow, there is the search for joy and ultimately, the attainment of joy. We become light, refreshed, as if we have wings. Even in sorrow, even in happiness—finding and finding joy is the beauty of life.

FULL OF JOY

If you know the art of living, life is joy in every situation. No sadness, no sorrow, just happiness. What can a mind filled with sorrow achieve? Nothing at all. Fill yourself with joy. Love yourself, give yourself time. We have to live smilingly in every situation, live like a swan. If the mind is pure and simple, joy automatically bursts forth from within, radiates.

CONSCIOUSNESS IS BLISS

Consciousness is bliss, unconsciousness is sorrow. Even in consciousness, we will have to go through sorrow, because we have accumulated sorrow, but it has to be broken; fear will not help. We have made lies sweet, truth bitter - so that lies can work. This is self-deception. We shoot arrows with open eyes, in the light, yet the arrows do not hit the target. Because we do not work in consciousness. The work done in consciousness, gives happiness as well as joy.

LIVE IN JOY

Happiness is not somewhere outside, it is within us. We should express the meaningful and the best in life. We should not take any decision in anger or trouble. We should not share sorrow and trouble with anyone. This will reduce happiness. Share love, spread happiness, we will be happy. If I am not happy, it means that we do not know how to live. We should change the direction of life. Happiness is raining within us every moment, we should live in it.

PEARLS OF JOY

We are special, unique, incomparable. Let us become calm, silent. Let us become absorbed in the song of our inner music, and then no external noise will be heard. There is no commotion inside. Dive into your inner self, and pearls of joy will rain down. Find the treasure within you. Become your own.

PRAYER

Prayer arises unconsciously in a heart free from vices, pure and calm, a call comes from the heart. Prayer is a good intention; prayer contains the power of the mind and the strength of devotion. Prayer always talks about self-interest and the welfare of all. Prayer is not associated with any negative energy. Prayer is surrender. Surrender contains freedom and liberation. Liberation contains joy and a feeling of fulfillment. Prayer makes the impossible possible; miracles come to fruition.

GRACE AND JUSTICE

Always trust in God's grace and justice. Surrender your circumstances, your sorrows, and pain to God. Make Him your best friend. Be patient and don't lose heart; He will surely show you the way. If our intentions are clear and our goals are right, God will surely help us in some way. The world's transformation and destruction occur according to the laws of nature. Therefore, be assured that whatever is happening is good, and whatever will happen will also be good. May we remain happy and joyful.

BESTIALITY AND DOMINANCE

Between animality and dominance, we must first attain humanity, so that we can journey towards dominance. Our deformity is our animality. This is where the sorrow and stress lie. Increase respect for humanity, remove the impurities from your heart, and live a righteous life. May we become blooming roses, whose fragrance fills the entire atmosphere with joy and allows our inner consciousness to take concrete form. May we share the nectar of life with enthusiasm and affection.

SHOULD NOT REMAIN INCOMPLETE

We should not remain incomplete; we are seeds, it is our right to become trees. May we become what we came to be. Let life blossom and flourish. Let the fragrance of our existence spread. May our personality and life become so integrated into our being that our silence becomes vocal, intense, and showers peace. And our small sky and tiny piece of land begin to seem infinite. May we become a witness, a seer, simply observing the world and its heartbeats.

HAVE FUN CELEBRATION

A pure mind always walks the path of truth. Truth resonates in the heart as prayer. Compassion and friendship find their place in the mind. Then an inner music is heard. The very presence of truth in life is a celebration of joy. So celebrate, dance like the waves of the ocean, sing like the birds, bloom like flowers, spread fragrance. All of nature is celebrating joy. We too should celebrate, experience the supernatural divinity.

WORDS BECOME PRAYER

Our voice, our words are a divine blessing. Words have infinite power and strength. Remember them in every situation, in every circumstance. Let us follow them. Words should not remain mere words but should become prayers, chants. Words should become mantras, good resolutions. Speech should become a veena, life should become a celebration. Our words should become medicine, a prayer. Words should infuse life with nectar and shower love.

THE INNER JOURNEY BEGINS

Understanding the mystery of life, we become seekers of truth. Walking on the path of truth-meditation, we immerse ourselves in silence and bliss. Life is definitely a garden of flowers - let us be overwhelmed by its fragrance, let us gaze sensitively at the matchless, indescribable beauty of life. Let us be filled with wonder and become ecstatic with the brilliance and glow of the countless colours and forms of life. Let the language of love, the echo of silence fill our hearts with emptiness. Let us let our existence be vocal. Let the inner journey begin, let life become a celebration and let us attain our inner glory.

We are God's signature, our value cannot be diminished unless we want it. We were priceless, we are priceless, and we will remain so.

Pratibha Jain

Life introduction

Life itself is the greatest school. The desire in life is to remain a lifelong student. In this vein, Pratibha possesses deep experience in examining and studying the thoughts and emotions of the human mind. She has also had years of special interest and experience in meditation. This work is the essence of this, filled with positive sentiments. In this book, Pratibha has simply expressed how we can make life happier, better, and more valuable. Through this, we can view life as a solution and feel at ease and light.

"A disorder-free mind - a disorder-free life" is the music of life, "We should live in awareness, not in burden", this is the powerful story of life.

Pratibha has been a student of philosophy and is an excellent teacher of meditation. Her spirit is one of service. She also provides counseling, and spirituality is Pratibha's hallmark. At the age of 57, this is her first book being published. It is a unique product of her years of experience. Pratibha lives in Jaipur with her sons, Gautam and Siddhant, and her husband, Ajit Jain.

www.ingramcontent.com/pod-product-compliance
Lightning Source LLC
LaVergne TN
LVHW070909210926
848482LV00017B/1032